The Binding Dance

William Pruitt

For Pam

ACKNOWLEDGMENTS

Adelaide Literary Magazine: "What Am I Doing, Why Am I Here," "Varieties of Light," "To Welcome a Gift," "The Strange Motion of October 2020"

Anderbo.com: "Manhattan"

Kestrel: "The Binding Dance"

Last Leaves: "At the End of the Day"

Leaping Clear: "Crow and Moon (Not Shown)," "Belief"

Literary Juice: "How Things Look"

Off-Course :"You Don't Have To Count," "How to Tell your Lover's Not a Robot," "The English as a Second Language Teacher Explains Question Words."

Otis Nebula: "Travelers"

A Plate of Pandemic: "When Everything Gets Back to Normal" and Late Fall 2020."

Poets Speak: "We Care More Now"

The Ravensperch: "Magic & Community"

Sick Lit: "What We Do"

Steel Toe Review: "The Old Life".

Stone Boat: "Changing Trains in Motion"

Tellus: "What If"

Bold Cities and Golden Plains (FootHills press): "Joplin"

Walking Home from the Eastman House (self-published): "Manhattan," "Oak Orchard," "The War on Crickets," "Running Naked Outside," "The Very Thing That Saves Us."

Contents

I.

Opening Statement

When you make a poem, give.
Give plentifully, if for no other reason
Than that your arms, open for giving,
May receive what poem gives back.

God is not you or I, nor a version of us.
Neither does God exalt or debase me or you.
To immerse ourselves in human beings
Is not to be limited to human beings

The Great Tree
The Sacred Fire
Are not ideal forms
Not ideals, not ideas

You Don't Have To Count

You don't have to count the syllables in this line
or apprehend a complex rhyme scheme
there's nothing bothering me, I'm not angry
and I have no lost brother or loved one who has recently died.

My leafy street is a riot of scarlet and gold just now
but I don't expect you to visualize it, nor do I hope
you will see a droid army, or fairies or elves marching
down the street in a huff. No burning or smoldering in my soul

if I had one. If the Devil says, "Pruitt?" I'll just say "Here!"
This poem may end up 14 lines, or maybe twelve, but there's no need
to count those either. You are free. I release you from caring
& calculating. Any more than you already do is too much.

Haunted

I'm asking a question and so far no one has answered

It's not like Socrates asking is such and such an action virtuous
nothing like that

my question is *who?*

Every story
from *It's a Wonderful Life* to *Divina Commedia*
to *Journey to the End of the Night*
is about who
and is haunted by who
and by mentioning these stories I have swirled around more
ghosts
who are haunted by each other and themselves
until they find their place in the tale

transparencies of ourselves
we place over the grid of the story
and it all comes right
there's the master
there's the one out of control

courtship is there
a breezy lunch with friends
the one who set herself up for failure
the one who was cast out, justly or not
the one who always lit up the room, or settled it

the story that has us all in there
who are all who here

the story that keeps us from killing ourselves
over the fact of having consciousness

If I were to tell you dear friend the very thing
you find cause for suicide is the greatest miracle
you might ask how I know that

my answer is I don't know
how, but I know

Magic & Community

share an experience,
strike a bond,
precious thing

but when we practice Magic,
(which includes all art)
whatever bond is struck
is incidental to something else.

On the other hand
the way we form groups
is not magic, but magical

like birds on a power line until
the group acquires a not-
group to be defined by.

and mingling becomes
defiled with meaning and manipulation
which blight the bond

social buffering hardens
 into law, which falls
under the will of those

who think the immaculate
sphagnum ground
cricket that is the universe

is a machine.

Thus do we invoke Magic
(which includes all art),
to keep the cell walls permeable
restore the sacred power of touch

The Sickness of Goals

I.

cardinal
carols the dawn,

sparrows' irregular song

printer's light
blinks every
two point nine seconds

II.

In the old days
Original Sin.
these days,
what are your goals.
a house in the country
a dog and a family
a bronze statue of Kali?
Or are you a lazybones
kill dad fuck mom kind of guy?
Darwin never said
it was just about survival.

Two Sisters

You say you didn't force her, but there is
so much about this we can't know.
Did she really have a chance to say she would tell
her sister, your wife? Is that what pushed you
out of the black, into the void? Or was it all one wave
of rage, your hands closing around her neck your true release?
You have sundered a connection. You have no voice here.

I want instead to speak with you, dear girl, gone these seven
years.
I did not know you. He was my student years before.
It must have come up suddenly, the snowy day,
the cold house, you there visiting, your sister was out
when he came in. The end of your life came faster
than you thought it would, a man's face

without any human there, with only
intent to annihilate. But you're here
and you can hear me. I want to know
what it was like to die that way. You might not
have had a chance to scream. Was it a breath the living
can't imagine being the last that showed you for the first time

the angel who had always been there? Did you have time to think
you'd been right to be afraid, you always knew
he hated blossoms? You made a leap then,
over the states of bearing fruit and slow
decline, carrying the outlines
of unworldly bloom and grace.

And you dear sister, how many days have you
excoriated yourself for bad decisions, starting with the marriage,
all the way to being out of the house when he came home.
Hatred obliterating the boundaries of your heart since then,
the way they had to hold you back when the police took him
for his sentencing, your hoarse screams churning the tainted air.

It's easy to say she was good, and you have taken her inside
and now feel her there. But I know there's a world where
numbers are real and every day you wake up and know
that it is *her* this happened to, not someone you didn't know
or knew a little, but one you grew up with, shared a room with,
had a place for in your heart that's now a tomb.

like it was you in that room on that day,
you who fell under the Sword of Damocles,
only your death is long and daily, choking
in its own bile, not like hers at all. I hope
you've found her. I don't mean in your mind or heart
or some *there* you can't get to from here except to die.

I'm talking about climbing out of the deep hole of your beaten self
and clasping the links that change this hell game.
Links you have to let go of her hand to find, if you can get past
the ringing murders in your mind to where the cold hard
ground is cloud, the roots go all the way through! The flowers on
this end—
I mean the real ones— are waiting for you to know what they are.

Bad Neighborhood

Almost before he knew what lust was
he would think about a girl he knew in school he saw
in his rough and scary stray dog neighborhood
hanging out on the corner in the evening with boys

He imagined her sitting on his lap
in her nightie. But what he dared
not dream of was the practice
of hanging out with people.

In his family, you needed a reason to be with others
and a time to be back. They were never
late for church, where man was so weak he had
to get himself in front of Jezebel so he wouldn't

have to look at her from behind.
And all that quoted chapter and verse
was a ramshackle dam on a rogue river.
No dancing! No casual touching! Best not to have

A close female friend who is not a potential mate.
In bed he conjured a companion, a sister, a friend.
In the tub he learned to jack, which took away
some tension but left the loneliness.

This is the way the foisted world-view got confirmed
where he could see women only in relation to himself,
missing out on true relation, got the bait & switch:
look but don't touch. Don't believe what you see. Don't

imagine too much. He thought
he was going places but he kept coming
to a cul de sac where people make you uncomfortable
when they look at you when you're looking at them.

He never learned of the boulevard of dreams that led to
a grand roundabout the next street over

Running Naked Outside

He would wait until it was dark. Until his parents weren't home. When there was wet snow on the ground. When the streets were cold and quiet.

There was a Baptist church across the street, with a classroom annex. There was an alley behind it, where he walked to school. He would go down into his basement, where the garage was. There he would take off his clothes and race across the street. Running fast as he could, wet snow on his feet sending chills up his body. But the excitement kept him from feeling any cold inside. The cold was only on the outside. When he got to the annex, he would huddle behind a corner, looking first at his house across the street, and then, all around him. He could be seen now, if anyone looked.

No one was looking. So he ran back, back to the open doors of the garage, faster than ever, faster naked than clothed, so naked and fast that he was hardly there, desire that couldn't be held down, couldn't even be seen, a comet with a trailing tail of indefinite, ineffable boldness, falling across the unwatched sky of the subterranean suburb.

Live Free or Die!

The reason why
We so resist
Having our will
Imposed on
By someone else

Is because we
Spend our lives
Imposing our will
On someone else

The Binding Dance

for Pam

That day the stranger at the airport spoke about
his work, his family, the baby he lost,
his wife's lifelong grief at not seeing the body,
you say you felt your father talking to you,
and you ask me what would a person
who didn't believe in a soul make of this?

Well, how about a spinning carousel, each of us
spinning too, the way planets move with the sun
in its great precession around something around
something around, a vastness we can express
and shape if we don't get dizzy from the turning.
Maybe we're unspooling slowly as we spin,

maybe that's why things seem familiar but different.
Hey, if we're looking at this whole thing through
a mirror— the way it's been since we dropped the vision
quest and replaced self-knowledge with self-exile, a tic
picked up in adolescence, now a virus— our
perception's bound to be buckled.

We think it's time that makes us grow, but maybe
the beat we keep is not the clock's. The instant
we notice our breathing's not controlled by time
but lives within it like a house, that instant
everything changes. It's then we see how time is a
magician's trick that makes us blink

while our mind wrinkles. What if it's *now*
your father's there, and babies, briefly alive.
It's gravity and centrifugal force that make
it all *seem* old. You don't need to imagine a soul
if angels interact through those
countless filmy expanding contour lines,

if we refuse to let the social noise we make,
the great religions of Time and Self, cover up
what's happening in front of our eyes.
It's easier to think it's gone, but nothing's gone.
The footings your father sank for his foundation
turned instantly to legend when he died.
Meanwhile, meanwhile, meanwhile, meanwhile,
that expenditure of moments we call our life
is a ceaseless dance that binds it all together with
ropes of light like Wonder Woman, till we need a break.
If you ask, what happens to me when I die, back at you, Dear.
Who dies?

The Old Life

Remember when you activated your cell phone and it showed the old time for an instant before switching to current time, do you know what that really is?

It is a sleeping soldier supposed to be on guard duty, standing at attention when the
officer walks in.

It is the old life, the old attitudes, hanging on when you thought they were gone.

It is the master magician, getting caught with his wand down—he almost let you see time is an artifice.

II.

Brightness Emerging

Still dark when I drive to the Y, the first Halloween lights,
Front yard election signs — Carbone, Proietti, DiNolfo—
Leaving the dream of Italian Irondequoit for the city,
I move invisible through dawn
In the clear air at the beginning of autumn

Traffic lights swing out in the dark:
Perpetual green arrow where St. Paul veers right
Green lights of Thorndyke and Titus,
Road curves, mimics river's contours to the west

There are people in the crepuscular light
They wait, city bus, school bus
They have gotten themselves out of sleep to this place
Where they must be still again

I cross the river at Driving Park
The door of the Y with the light still on looks
Different now with a glow in the east,
People move inside the old brick building,
Shapely woman leaves the barbells says hi
To Willie, wiry and compact at eighty,
Who feels her way into the donut weights.

I work pull down, leg press, leg extension, abdominal
Y   M   C   A red lit letters spread
Wide across second floor wooden wall
Bikes with mounted tv screens,
Windows showing pearl-colored sky

Sugar maple goes olive in sunrise
Pale winged seedlings carry the cycle,
Rose garden brightens across the street,
Red and pink flowers on the last day of summer
White squares are cards marked with varietal names
Dick Clark   Sunsprite   Sutter's Gold

Joplin

The summer I graduated from high school in suburban St. Louis,
I worked as a laborer for a small construction company. The
boss had a small plane so he could take bids on jobs other
companies wouldn't bother with, far out of the city, sometimes
out of the state, fly us out Monday and bring us back Friday
night. I had been going with my first serious girlfriend for a year.

I remember the second summer of our affair
I was working in Joplin, flying home weekends
The warm Friday nights
O, miles before we met I would see her...

Her browned body spread over my dreams
Like a great crab that has swallowed the sun
And her white breasts and hips were like bold
Cities rising from golden plains

At the End of the Day

My son calls me up to tell him goodnight. He is four.
I ascend the stairs, he is already in bed with Teddy.
He asks me to sing him the song I made up for him.
I sing it every night. It has birds and fish and sun and stars,
trees and rivers and mountains.
It comforts both of us, a routine to end the day.
To tell a story of how each member
of our family loves him, how he loves them back.

As I sing and we both listen, I am allowed in this moment
to step away from *son*— he's not just that— but
another human being, deliciously close.
Together we make a life.
It has an arc, a story, a poem, a song.

I know I am young, going somewhere wonderful
But it will never be any better than this.

At Hogback Mountain

The lithe Japanese grandfather takes his time,
his progeny scattered on the walkway
lets the view usurp his speech,
his thoughts become vowels
at the back
of his tongue
at the sight of those tightly

bunched florets of russets and yellows and golds,
here and there a conifer strip of green, how they
extend mountains into sky and valley
further than we thought bright color could go with line.

biker couples at the Hogback Mountain scenic overlook,
get their picture taken in the big chair,
"won't be able to get out" said the tall one,
Yemeni women swathed in drapery,
German girls with short skirts and calf-high white socks,

Readers at a marker asked to imagine a journey in 1804
Bennington to Brattleboro in a close coach,
darkness coming soon, road ruts becoming mud,

all of it ours.

Spring

Trimming the mock orange
and detaching vines, I feel
a thought wrap itself around my work,
we're in a lucky pocket I think
as the wind picks
up the ragged blue tarp
which I'm about to burden
with sticks & branches,
flips it, rippling, and suddenly

a kite from another time appears in a blue sky,
or maybe it's a flag or a curtain or a shirt,
something soft & blue the wind could
billow through, and what if

hope is not something added on, but part of seeing,
as I patiently separate the wisteria from the mock orange
because
no matter how far I cut back hope to try to see the
real thing, there is still hope.

Frames

for Joel Bloom!

Some people we feel lucky
To have in our lives.
When they die, we live.
We think: that dear one hasn't changed.
By which we mean his life with us
Is a framed portrait
Too late to paint.

But it doesn't seem quite right
To say he's dead. What we mean is,
He's disappeared.
Where did he go?
What did he leave,
This thing *I'm* in?
We're in a universe
With a boundary.

It isn't like he was never here.
The leaves are different colors, depending on what angle
To the sun we see them, but he's the same from every angle,
With his Sephardic curls, his young and sallow face,
His wise and sparkling old man's eyes. I still love him,
Present tense. What do I love?

How Things Look

A thin strand of
Horizontal cloud
Across the lower
Half of a full moon
After a night of rain:

A hair out of place?
The thrill of her
Letting you see her
As she is

Beautiful

1.

Why do I need to tell Petra she is beautiful? (I don't tell her.)

Petra has some kind of deliberate wantonness, a bravado, a
sudden distance.
Chewing gum, she says, I don't care, the hell with everything.
Not passion, a relaxed and defiant indifference perversely
attractive.
It comes with an unexpected sigh. Petra, with her
Small upturned nose, eyes that gleam abruptly, lightup smile.

I haven't seen her for two years, and here she is.
What kind of a link do I hope to forge by telling her she is
beautiful?
She probably just got a nose job and dyed her hair.
She would think I'm a Pavlovian dog for drooling.

What kind of a cul de sac does her beauty represent?
A bright thing in a darkened place.
Is beauty a hole in truth's pocket?

2.

I'm conflicted by the story in Zen Flesh, Zen Bones, about the
beautiful woman who burns her face in order to be accepted by
her teacher.

On the one hand, there's the freedom to destroy, to rearrange, to
SHAPE.

But where is respect for NATURE.

Does the teacher reject her because of her beauty, or because
she is beautiful?

Is beauty a hole in truth's pocket?

3.

No beauty
No truth
No teacher

Belief

Some have stopped caring, some say it's a joke,
the way mother plays
peek-a-boo, then goes away forever.
Some lean a ladder of belief against
that place she disappeared
and feel it steady, or shrug off
whether it is steady or not.

You may think you have your own little corner
especially if you live near streets and intersections
You may think sinister controlling agents turn
the wheel, and it's only a matter of time before
the earth is covered with concrete and stillness and
masks and it doesn't matter if the mask
is smiling or frowning it's a mask, but then perhaps

you also believe time is a big familiar arch you live under?
That you are fixed in place by your genes and credit rating and
coordinates?
That the tree falls silent in the empty forest?
(What tree? What forest?)
That an ending is anything more
than someone's decision to stop?

None of these things is true
but all of them
are easier to accept
than the meandering parade
everybody's in that stretches to the horizon

Nothing Remarkable

There's nothing remarkable about my life.
It has the same contours as yours.
It might have more sex, or less.
It might have more or fewer wives or husbands

but believe me, it's not that different.
I mean, maybe you haven't been to Bryce Canyon.
Maybe you've climbed K-2, perhaps you even
have brothers and sisters, but still. It's pretty much the same.

Of course, if we've rubbed elbows,
joined hands, caressed or comforted each other
then you know the lab test for comparisons
was contaminated long ago

August at the Peabody

It's the grand lobby: fine-etched plaster overhead painted to look
like wood
second floor mezzanine on the perimeter where guests can stand
and look down,
in the middle of it a fountain, solid block of Italian travertine with ducks
a dozen well-spaced massive granite pillars enclose the lounging
zone with bar

a space buzzing with social energy, lubricated by drink and ducks
who live on the rooftop where one can see all of Memphis
none of it would make the grade without Philip Joyner at piano in
one corner,
playing Maple Leaf Rag, Liszt, Apologize by One Republic,

always there, playing when you step out into the heat and walk
down to the river,
playing when you come back in and touch the cool marble, just like
someone said about Monk, the music is always going on,
even when he isn't there, even when the piano plays itself

even when they knocked the building down and built another one,
the sounds he makes not extra or complementary, but light that shines
on why all this is: music entwined with talking, like vines on
marble columns,
reminding us against fear and hatred that we are beautiful
together.

III.

Manhattan

Busy Starbucks Midtown, young family quickly
settles itself around a little table,
the daughters look 7 and 9, have long coats.
Mother goes off with the younger.
The older holds a small dog & says to her father,
"You're a better cook at lunch and Mommy's
a better cook at dinner, do you agree?" Years later,
that girl expresses her anger. The mother says,
"But what about that Friday after Thanksgiving,
remember we sat in that Starbucks at Broadway and Bond?
Don't you remember how happy we were?"
Around the blue eye of the mother turns the city,
countless pairs of eyes drift like tumblers with lost keys.

Who can hold it all together.
Who will come sit with me at this table.

The War on Crickets

I'm sitting under a tree, just like Buddha,
A roar comes toward me through the fog
Cement mixer extra loud with the two motors,
Big white rotating cylinder tagged
With nine eleven flag, which means something
Different from before we invaded Iraq.

Pickup truck glides across the campus lawn,
Smashing innumerable crickets to bathe
Hanging petunias on the standing lamps
In a nutrient spray. A friend comes over
To talk. I put pen and paper away.

The sun obliterates the fog.
I teach English all day
To Mexicans, Dominicans, Hondurans, Salvadorans,
Teenagers on a break from high school where they
Tough it out among monolingual Americans

I eat a sandwich for dinner.
Back at the tree, I see a broad,
Settled valley, and evening sun
Pass slowly across the wooded plain.
Shadows inch eastward, bringing
True form to steeple and stone

July 2007

The English as a Second Language Teacher Explains Question Words

First of all, let's get one thing straight:
What is actually *how*, all scrunched up. OK?
When you say *what*? I have to *show* how.
So vocabulary will only take you so far.

And *where* must include *when*, for the traveler
Who thinks the dark road he took before dawn
Is the same one he comes home on in bright day,
Just because the sign says *19*, is mistaken.

Who is -er: travel-er, teach-er, you and I.
As for that last one, don't worry.
Except for mistakes, anomalies
And betrayals, there is no *why*.

Oak Orchard

small spider climbs up the side of the observation deck
first fly buzzes by
blue propeller plane heron drone
wings fold & lights
swamp frogs & peepers vertigo

does all this end at death or
is this the what (or maybe
it's death in this, musical),
(or maybe that's a different).
In the concert of birds and more birds,
heron flies over, legs dipping slightly
my wife lies on her back on the unfinished planks
midriff exposed to sun from just below
the navel to where the ribs begin

pond is rimmed with cat tails and trees
with not yet leaves
she takes her boots off, her feet's raw places feeling
sun
car glints through bare woods
peepers pick up again

a car, these words, got us here
so she can turn on her side and I
can see her voiced protected refuge heron sigh

What Are Years

for D.C.

What are years? Nothing,
I spin them out of a shuffled deck, one as good
as another, 34 no more than 14 or 4 or *4*.
History is smoke. I clear it away, take
your hand, look you in the eye,
across the decades.

A brief flash
so much to talk and laugh,
then flame went out,
by me, looking for closeness
got mortified by a letter
with underlined words
I understand it now
What I saw in your eyes
was part of the figured spinning top
my role was to keep going, not stop.

But you taught Regard,
allowed me to look at you,
not to stand off or gaze separate, but
feel the bonds grow intolerably deep,
how seeing makes more than what is there.

Now I see
what is not there
your face is exactly the same as it was
and I don't even know if you

had the child you were trying to have,
your prominent slim
nose and deep set eyes facing
the smoky, unimaginable future.

How to Tell your Lover's Not a Robot

How do you know I am not a robot?
How do you know these lines are not composed by algorithm?
Is it my job to convince you I'm a human being?
What does it mean if I sound *convincing?*

The leaves of autumn are turning and
the human hides among them.
Now you must stop looking at me and ask
yourself, what am I? Have you already decided?
Is what or who you are not part of the changing field you play
on?

Don't try
to beat Deep Blue. Don't ask anything
from your lover. To look her in the eye
while you hold her is to toss
the coin in the empty well.

Don't let the sound you don't hear
of it hitting bottom be because
either one of you stopped listening.

The Gates

I.

Looking into her eyes
Was to see into her scene,
Her tastes, her taste, her prompts,
Her other, her weather,
You thought, *here is something different.*
But how could it shore up?
How could the soft hair on her
Arms even risk appearing *here*?

II.

Now she's gone and gets
Your heartsick blame
As if misplacing her
Was her fault
As if she was about nothing
But your pain.
If you look at the world
From your wound,
You see wound.
If you look at the world
With your wound in it
You see blemish, not a stain

III.

Now you know she was not
Better than the world
She was the *window*, fool
You got stuck on her pane.
She was there so you could more
Clearly see this every day thing.
She was the gates, to more cleanly enter
This life you have, not another.
The scene you saw in her eyes
Was who you were to her on the clearest days.

Raisin

A man has lived in proximity to women
without getting entangled with them, he thinks.
(Sun on the hillside, grapes slanting lakeward.)
This is what men need, he thinks.
To be around women without getting enmeshed.
But what does it mean to be *around* women?
Aren't we always? Whether we want to be or not?

A man thinks he is not entangled
(Each grape taking what sun gives).
But what does that mean? Is it about not being juicy
with each other, not sharing stickiness?
Or is it to not brush skin, smell hair, back of neck?
Or is it to not revolve around each other in space?
"Here comes my baby...Never to be mine ♫"

How can I say "a man has lived?" What do I know
about *a man*? What about a real baby?
Here comes a man now, shirtless, walking slowly
down a street holding a tiny baby getting hair,
getting a head big enough to hold space.
I dove into that, I made that baby my star
until it was time to let her go.

A man lives, immersed. The distance
from a to b in his life just grows until it's gone.
He says, I believe everything happens for a raisin.
He looks for what the sun revolves around.
He knows there's no way
to diagram the sentence of sex.
His bumper sticker says *I brake for brightness*

The Very Thing That Saves Us

We get together after I've been a couple of days away
our conversation as usual like finding
the stones that will keep our feet dry
as we cross the cresting brook

but you've got something to tell me and it comes out indirectly
it turns out while I was gone you died, fell from a height or
something
so this conversation we're having is a fire built on tinder
and I'm the only one of us growing older

and when I ask how far you fell
you say you let your insurance lapse
I say, *I didn't ask about insurance,*
I asked how far you fell

Raven Talk

Ravens have gathered in the old cedar grove
To express delight at white
Dawn again fading in & this time
With first quarter moon

They have their own word for February, which includes
Their word for home, which we call Death Valley,
Where mountains now emerge in profile from the dark.

The birds whirr, rasp, coo and coax their own
Silhouettes into definite form, then go quiet,
For even they have no word for what
Is coming over the Grapevine Mountains

Changing Trains in Motion

Bobby Militello at the Lovin' Cup 12/20/15

A few of us willing to have our thought trains replaced
by polyrhythms in melodic sequence have gathered
at the Lovin Cup to sit below two half-circle ceiling
drop downs swathed in corrugated tin to listen to
the Fat Man and his friends talk to each other
using strings and sticks and stops

When he plays, his bulk leaves him and he gambols,
like a fawn or a young girl through a field of buttercups
or up a trellis he twines with his sax
followed by the guitarist and bassist and drummer
and when he plays flute, he grows even lighter,
as this holiday crowd begins to change trains

from their own track which was rapidly running out
to this different one which just keeps going, all of us
in the air, our mass supported by nothing but vine,
musicians thinking out loud, infinite thought quantified
by practice, then re-enchanted by sleight of hand, when Bobby
switched his bulk for grace without it being noticed

What If

What if I say a constricting snake,
Bound with stars & studded
With gold hasps, strains to bursting,

& Looking through the moving water
For an instant you see a shape below
That makes everything mean something else

IV.

All Night

crickets and katydids of late summer go on all night beneath
dripping trees
you can't see the full moon for the clouds
there are others in the world besides me
there is nothing in the world that is not happening to someone

is this toad someone? what about the rock it sits on?
is the sum of someones equal to something like time?
does the Buddha dog's bark make a sound in the empty junkyard?
whatever's beyond you and me is right here

The Making of Joplin

Between deliveries on the loading dock
back of the Penney's no longer there
big door open, pen in my hand
watching snowflakes fall on the parking lot
and the weed-choked stone of the abandoned canal,
thinking back to that summer I graduated from high school
when I dropped from the sky into sundry podunk towns,

Small company, boss had a little plane so he
could bid on jobs— curbs, rest stops, freezers
in places too small too far for bigger firms' concerns.
He'd bring a couple of carpenters and me, the laborer,
Sometimes he'd let me take the yoke while we were in the air

Swooping down in the middle of a cornfield;
putting up a freezer for Ralston Purina
Big Paul McCowan leading the way
finishing cement, laying tile
wide white overalls pockets drooping
sixteen penny nails in his teeth ,
they pounded the floor all day not stopping
we worked past every diner's closing time but one

I missed my girl & thought of her on the hottest days,
at night in the busted AC fleabag Postville motel,
we built a freezer inside a cooler one week in Rolla
came out in the evening heat for an hour felt cool
how many times I called her from the pay phone
outside the Blue Gardenia in Joplin, looked up

through the glass booth while we talked & saw
her smiling form sublime among the stars

And when my work was done she was in the Bahamas
I was preparing for college, shopping for clothes at Korvette
The days already cooling down .

So I wrote a poem on the loading dock with the door open &
called it Joplin

We Care More Now

"Get em outta here!" Donald Trump, at campaign rally, 2016

Once there was a country made itself into
a giant pyramid scheme, it worked
for a while as long as the ones at the bottom
kept believing, but as people forgot
how to think, the promises in the chain letter
became incoherent and the ones not far from the bottom
started to panic and demand their share and in their fear
they lost empathy, their only real treasure
and connection to the great world
> *Get em outta here*

So no more making nice in civil discourse
the rich who made the poor more poor
started helping them to hate the poorer yet
(though some realized a Chernobyl of collective hate
with no OFF switch *might* be a mistake)
but the refrain began and would not stop
Someone was responsible for no flavor in the bread,
no joy in Sunday hymn
> *Get em outta here*

They never mattered except to build the country
now they complain, now they want *more*
it's not enough we let them in
it's not enough we gave them freedom
they think they're special

they don't understand American Exceptionalism,
they'd find out if they were in North Korea:
                    Get em outta here

The ones at the top have a game that the ones below
don't know about. Let's play
grow up in a ghetto.
Let's play
tie your hands behind your back now shake my hand.
Let's play
the shadow game.
We'll pretend you are equal to me.
You can use my water fountain. We'll even
swim in the pool together! But can you see
the shadow of your skin in my smile?
You missed it game over!
                    Get em outta here

Some say this hate is
what we've come to.
but think about it

slaves have been around
since before the pyramids
we were just too busy being afraid
to care too much about that,
too busy being needy
around that strong man
with the whip

but it just so happens
there are enough of us
who care more now

than we could or did
at the scary pyramids.

We care more now about the ones
from the next neighborhood
the ones next door
they are not equal to us because
 they are not numbers and neither
are we. They are human beings
and we care more now than we used to.

Every Spring

after Joseph Campbell's *Primitive Mythology*

magnolia with new leaves,
dead branch hanging

Long ago kings had term limits
at the end of a cycle, say seven years
they were buried, burned or sometimes
expected to hack themselves to pieces

sparrows under my dormer
nest-building noise

someone remembered metaphor
more meaningful to just act it out

meanwhile working folk still had to
fight actual wars and die

bluebells crocus skunk cabbage
flowers in the sucking mud

then people said how about if we do that too
how about if we all be artists
this was not acceptable to kings
who responded by making an example
of holding on for life

> *she makes a necklace of dandelion*
> *flowers, she makes a crown*

Yahweh still needs the smell of burning flesh,
& the sight of spilled blood, still smites Cain
for offering green, who goes fratricidal every
day of the world IS LITERAL all the holy
scriptures scream, NO TIME BUT CLOCK TIME insist
the strategists of war, and God said from
a burning bush that children
are the only ones who blush

> *Beyond the cycle blood smoke wheel*
> *every spring she makes the dandelion crown*

What We Do

"The most sublime act is to set another before you."
William Blake, *Proverbs of Hell*

We want to be loved not
for our talents or skills
but for who we are,
for what we do,
which *is*
who we are

Others might think,
if they don't pay attention,
that what we do
is fill out the blank spaces
in their lives
with our skills and talents
instead of making moving
holes in their world composed
of neither self nor other.

The wise woman knows that she does not know me
until she sets me before her. And there I am.
This is not about deference or hierarchy.

The best we can do in this world
is to set others before us
even when
they pretend we're not there
If they deem

our constructions unsatisfying
our diversions unsuccessful
it's probably because
they haven't yet guessed
that's not what we do

Travelers

Remember when we were travelers,
and it took time to do things?
That's all time was back then.
We built fire, animals stepped
away, stories rose
and we
extended into things.
Right now, then,
I, myself,
standing on the North Rim
go fifteen miles out, in
to that little cleft. We all do, did, do.

Time was there were always plenty of gods to go around.
Time was, was no time, just an arc with a prize at the end,
and everybody had a power of who they were.
no pretend or trophies for first or second place.
We were the trophies. If we ate each other, it was in tribute.

Now we're stuck, everyone of us downsized,
spies reporting on each other to a Ghost Agency.
We don't extend so far,
not even to each other's shoulders.
Now we have a soul, or we did,
before they pulled that out too.

But things are easy these days. Not too much pain for
some. Water heaters, country cousins, gas grills.
Climate control, trucks with food porn on their sides.

The only real pain for everybody is
this time thing we've been gifted with,
and the soul, now held out in front of us,
as a mystery to see if it's *really there*.

Life Begins and Ends in Dream

1

 Two girls are with my sister and me when she discovers she has
tiny ants coming out of her eyes. I know that she will die of this,
the girls have told me. But they tell her if she does certain things
she will be okay. Yet I know it will all end differently.

2

Riding to England in a banana boat
sleeping in hammocks
U-boats in the waters around us

We were the 549th
In England we went up in gliders & C-47s for two weeks
so pilots could practice

Our units had eight machine gunners
In France we shot anything out of the sky ours or theirs
We spent a night in the forest with Panzer tanks
We lay low on a bluff, we heard but couldn't see
the destruction of Battery D

3

I took my son to Cobbs Hill when he was nine
to watch Jupiter take a comet that left a scar
liberating a few million megatons of energy
just like my dad helped liberate the French

We talked to Ed who bred springer spaniels
who once took an astronomy class at Cornell
—Two experiences changed my life, he said
Going to Glacier National Park
& seeing the crab nebula through the telescope in Ithaca.

4

A group of attractive, well-dressed women and men makes a silent appeal to a woman standing next to me on the street. Then they turn to me and do the same. Hands and fingers gesticulating rapidly, they implore me. Their energy is like fluttering birds. I don't know what they want me to do. It's a strange thing to look at someone directly in the eyes when they're not speaking. I look at a man. he is asking me, urging me to do something. What? What? What?

Objective Is Collective Subjective

"nothing either good or bad but thinking makes it so"
(*Hamlet* Act 2 Scene 2)

Thinking:

Overtime is time and a half
The day is already half-shot
For a Bills fan, all you can do is hope, etc.

Really? Not making any new neurons there, Bill
Lost in thought, you don't know where you are
Instead of saying "how are you"
We should say "where are you?"

Degrees of thought coherence:

1. Determining a thing is pleasant or unpleasant
♫ I'm watching my life today will I be happy or sad or
torpid or stupidj♫
2.. Determining a thing is good or bad
Fighting the devil is a good thing
Making a deal with the devil not sure
We want clean ins and outs
Cutting health care to the poor is evil
Accepting money from places you disapprove of...
3. Determining a thing *is*
Sunrise on THAT white oak on THIS June morning

But if we can't get to 3—can't agree on what IS or forget that
it's the highest form of thought
    — we get stuck on 2

The thought that forgets the living thing
The mask of rational that disguises fear
The voice of authority that throws its weight
The check on love that pretends to be clear

The trappings of the objective

Preparing to die, the master to his pupil: —You stink of Zen

True Objective is a social construct
True Objective is the inner life we've labored
                    approximately a million years to get to
Long time no see! Where *are* you?

Crow and Moon (Not Shown)

The soft rain that patters briefly
on my deck umbrella at dawn was
eons in the making. In fact,
its origins go back to
when the moon was made,
the same time this moist breeze,
riffling the top of the silver maple
which stands over me like
the tallest mountain, began.

Crow flies through this rain speaking to me
he finds a tree to land on

"I don't think you've heard this before."

"I won't say it again."

Duende

He tried to remember how it was before he had a family. Before his daughter was born. Before he crossed the Olentangy River. When it was getting colder where he was, when invisible fingers, streaked with gold were beckoning. He was thin and pale then when he imagined apples beyond the Olentangy River.

He was floating in a world of ice and quiet. He was savoring the sound of falling walnuts, the sight of distant lit-up windows. He was hearing music no one else could hear. His life felt light, like dice, he threw. He had a wife, she threw too. *Cross the Olentangy*, they came up.

There wasn't much to pack.

He had a gift, he didn't know what, for whom, he didn't know either. He thought he knew death and something death didn't know. He thought his life was lost, here take it, he said when they crossed the Olentangy River.

And something caught his eye. Those apples grew big and heavy on the boughs. People came back into form. He re-desired desire, he noticed his luminous wife was nubile, then gravid, then numinous.

The new world wasn't that different. It had some things he liked. And in his slow way, like a woman weaning her child, he left off sucking the world's tit. He wondered if he had already given the gift he had without noticing.

So now his daughter comes along, and her husband, the Scientist. —We carry around with us the sense of death, he tells them.

—I don't, said his son-in-law.

—Lorca called it Duende, he said.

—How do you know what happens when you die? his daughter asked.

—You imagine it, he said.

—So you're not saying it's true.

—It's like when you tell a story to children, (he was a storyteller), and afterward they ask you if it's true. And you answer, did it get your attention? And if they say yes, you can say, then it was real. And then you say, did you feel something here? (fist on heart) and if they say yes, you can say, then it was true.

—And what if they say, I will pray for you, said the son-in-law, who had a sense of humor.

—Then you say, prayer is a form of the imagination. All were pleased at this. But later, he understood that he was a different person from when he crossed the Olentangy River. It was not that he had to modify his beliefs, but that he could include the new people's perspective in his, for how could theirs not also be true.

He should approach the hidden world carefully, keeping the blades of the mind sharp as it parsed what is imagined from what is assumed. But he had seen the woman in robes shouldering the large clay urn in the desert by the spring.

V.

2020

Past Equinox

Where the boardwalk cuts across the marsh, sepia-toned river world is on both sides. I stand on a circular concrete slab that extends out from the boardwalk, and let the gulls and swans and ducks and heron be. Time of day when duck rumps are up as they feed by immersion and scooping. Heron has a different approach: wait. And thrust. These aren't just different species, these are different approaches to solving the first problem. They are spiritual states.

Yellowing cattails. This river's been here longer than the great lake child it feeds. Southerly breeze lets it all expand. Crickets trill. All this brilliance, here, now.

We've already reached
        the highest point
on the wheel.

Only in the plunge
do the reds and golds and bronzes
drive it home

Walking in Auburn

Chanda speaks to us outside the Seward House. She has a park ranger's uniform on: slim well-fitting pants, a ranger's shirt and broad-brimmed straw hat with leather band. Above a broad black mask, her dark bright eyes signify. Her long nappy braids trail past her shoulders to her badge. She has a gigaphone mic, and is here to tell us about the activities of African Americans in Auburn, and about the close relationship between the Sewards, William and Frances, and Harriet Tubman.

As we walk away from the spreading grounds, with its half mill wheels and hedges and raised beds and interconnecting paths, we hear about Neppie, the Newfoundland that Frances found as a stray puppy and brought home and raised. How he was poisoned with arsenic shortly after John Brown's raid on Harper's Ferry; and about the horses who died in the barn and carriage house, set on fire the year that Seward ran a presidential campaign as an Abolitionist.

We step out of history as we walk the street past the church that Harriet Tubman attended, with boarded up windows and charred bell tower, and the nearby house where Harriett's great grand niece still lives. We briefly step out of time into clarity, seeing emerge from the clearing mists the image of evil, laid out for a moment for all to witness: what was some people's quotidian, part of the furniture of the day, property you could sell, move around, reassign, touch; not something enclosed in a bible or Marvel Comics, but right here as visitors now get quiet and stop thinking and see.

Chanda carries herself with easy dignity and grace as we walk up to Fort Hill Cemetery, and look on Harriet's grave.

Trying to remember

    the mistakes we made

So we can get past

People like you and me caught

    In a system they grew up in.

    How did it get let in?

Knowing how it works isn't enough.

    You've got to vomit the arsenic.

Frances

Her husband wanted to negotiate the Fugitive Slave Act
She told him, don't settle with these people.
He knew enough to listen.
It wasn't just about Black people.

She named the dog Neppie, for Neptune.
He loved water. She lived through his death agony
But when they tried to assassinate her husband in his bed,

It was too much.

When Everything Gets Back to Normal

We're living in a bungalow
in Western Florida when Wolf Boy attacks.
My wife gets out of the house
while I distract

A second, larger
intruder joins the fray
we get in the car and tear down
the coast road past the causeway

We stop at someone's painted lady
to use the bathroom on the second floor
by the time we get to Dunedin,
word has spread about our home invasion

Everybody's talking about it as if we're not the only ones
we meet friends and go out for breakfast,
there's scattered diner talk, silverware reflecting
voices of amusement and anxiety

—Is Wolf Boy dead? —What about Skeleton Boy?
I keep thinking of the iris prints
in the stranger's bathroom
and the osprey nests atop power poles you could

see from the road we sailed down in terror.
When everything is normal will anything be left.
I say to the waiter, —Isn't it like
we're living in Dick Tracy?

We Are All Scientists

After the vaccine, we got out to see how the world had changed.
Some of our haunts for society and commerce had crumpled
Some of our loved ones were simply no longer there
That part of the toxic self hood that insisted
Night was Day and Closed was Open remained,
Compensating for what it had lost in numbers by
Cranking up volume, but the rest of us just observed what
Was going on around us. Which was a new birth.

We're skipping the part where we say, "I'm not a scientist."
We are all scientists now. We have learned how to ask questions.
Our hypotheses are tinged with dreams. We have a new
Scientific Method. Get a dream. Make your waking life
An experiment. Turn down the noise so you can hear the Voice.
Do what the Dream says. Check results. Repeat. Mind the Variables.

The Strange Motion of October 2020

Because no matter how much anticipation we feel
   or dread we fall prey to,
that won't count in the vote
Because this time is irreducibly before
Because a great black cat is coming
   through the mountain to our door
but we can't see her face till she reaches it
so we don't know if she'll be bringing
   the plague rat she's killed
or the cockatiel of promise

Because it is like
   the dream of the life we are living
which has the same length for the one alive
   whether we die tomorrow or in fifty years
Because we build furiously
   make foundations deep
and wonder if we will ever again be able
   to summon the same urgency
Because it doesn't matter how fast we go
Because all roads lead to the line for early voting

Because the beautiful trees
   are going on without us
Because we have stepped off
   the olive gold carousel,
glad it's still turning but not really on it this year

Because we are a hundred million-headed
   three year-old
who is building a tower of small blocks
Because the tower of babble rattles at us
   at our task,
choosing the path with heart

What Am I Doing, Why Am I Here

I dream I am playing a character whose actions I understand only as the story goes on. I am a powerful man who has my friends arrest a woman I am seeking revenge upon. A woman who loves me is with me.

I collect evidence on the arrested woman. It is then I understand what is happening, how the plot unfolds. I can see in my character's intensity and singleness of purpose that I intend to execute this woman for her misdeeds, and that this will surprise and horrify the woman who loves me, and she will resist, so the audience will have someone to root for.

"To be an error and be cast out is part of God's design"

William Blake

Metaphor Dog

Three of us are coming out of the theater, discussing a certain scene in the movie.

One of us says —The case couldn't have impressed the audience as it had no legal significance.

—I believe the whole purpose was the dog, I say.

(We had watched the dog appear to run out into busy night-time traffic, as if it were about to be hit. At a correction of perspective we saw the dog was on a leash, and a car stopped to allow the dog and its man to cross.)

— It was metaphorical, I say. Just as the Earth continues, so the dog almost got hit but didn't.

They seem satisfied by this, and the woman, relaxing into our collective embrace, says, —How is the Earth's axis, by the way?

—It is fine, I say. Just fine.

Late Fall 2020

Yesterday I walked down the long
hill toward the lake horizon,
Ontario moved inscrutably
northeast. So many leaves on the ground
whose little remaining color had leached out,
and legions of mares' tails in the western sky
curved firmly as if just brushed, preceded by
spaced paw prints overhead, their eastward
direction signifying the coming front.

This morning is gray and wet. Most of the leaves
of the Japanese maple briefly flake the old earth scarlet,
and the air is streaked with scattered gold.
We've choked so long on the cold directed against us,
what a breath of relief to find cold just being cold

Failure of Language

I'm standing on the balcony of my hotel room
talking to someone on the phone when I see
a fort explode in the distance, remnants coming
close to where I stand. We are being invaded.
Tanks pull up, soldiers enter the hotel.
I stop one. —What language do you speak?
He says, — I don't speak a language.
I think he misunderstood.
—No. no. I speak English.
What language do you speak?
His answer is the same.

White Tails

We have rested enough in our leafy bed
Now it's time for browsing till the cars start up
Apples that grow too high for this landowner to reach
And fall on this cracked black asphalt, and crack, are good.
No one knows we're here until they see us.
Then we stop. You look at us in groups.
When one of you says, *they are beautiful,*
We don't agree. When one of you says,
They are venison, we object.
Then we run, our white tails waving,
Leaping fences, cars, our own lives. We come to the
Dark mother we knew was there when we leaped.

Face in the Sky

Looking for the Northern Lights
We drive out to Hamlin beach.
The roads to beaches are closed.
We drive down a branch road
Where trees on both sides open to dark sky.

It's cloudy, but as we stand in the chilly air
Things slowly thin to haze overhead
Stars appear showing actual depth
The way a lover's true face
Emerges from the cumulus of years

There is a rippling to the northwest,
Clouds, or curved air?
Simplest black, or color before color?
Night birds cry, headlights
Send beams through bare woods.

Blue Jay

I am blue jay my din fills the suburban streets
When there's an open stem on this tube feeder
Among these buzzy scuffles and tiffs I grab it,
Ward off the sparrows with an evil eye

I won't join their unruly skirmishing
I reign here, like my brother corvid raven rules
The river valley and brother crow controls
The precincts of the city's trees and hills

The sparrows knock each other around all day
My baneful gaze declares one beak's thrust kills.
Flutter and fluff is the spirit of animation
Keep your distance, little birds, I say.

Gnostic Esoterica

(after K'naan's "In the Beginning")

We tell youth
they need the world
We say it does not need them,
we call that extreme capitalism.

We say we value them,
We don't tell them
that's another way to state
we like the way they taste.

We tell them they have to fight
and kill the world
for freedom, but the toxic flame
they must smother is at home

Wide Open

Here we are, people who have a strict communion
with God on Sundays and some days,
with folk who carry God like a reflective vest
and those with murder in their hearts for everything that moves
and those who come home and sit slack jawed,
and those whom Obama simply called unbelievers,
and those who neither believe nor disbelieve,

Isn't this how it's always been when the Word was not enforced
with chains or tablets, when the Evil Eye was not the most
feared chief in the village, when the Buzzard of Orthodoxy lifted
its talons just a little from the heretic's neck? When the enforcers
looked away and neurons bubbled up among those who did not know
what a fortunate period they happened to be living in:

Windows where we were free to imagine
the true afterlife, which might be
how we make it happen.
They're open wide right now
those Himalayas, sunk eight miles into the sea

Going to the Movies in Heaven

A couple have brought their kids to a movie.
It isn't really a kids film; more like Antonioni.
In the movie, a bird is flying around.

In the theater, doors are open to the warm spring day.
A sparrow flies in. People point, look, a bird.
Everybody's looking up. The man thinks

this is the kind of movie you have to pay attention
to every single detail. He puts his hand on his wife's back
and notices she isn't wearing a bra. She cranes her neck

to see the bird as it passes through the projector's beam.
It's like a pajama party, he thinks. The kids
are happy to be here.

He feels the sunlight coming into the darkened room.
He remembers they've ordered dinner to be delivered.
He wonders if they will remember to be at home.

To Welcome a Gift

"...The prince of stories
Who walks right by me..."
Velvet Underground, *I'm Set Free*

The sound of feet hurrying down the stairs: I will miss
my grandchildren this pandemic year, their faces shining out of
sleep,
older sister parceling out gifts for her brother and parents and
grandparents
when she could tear her attention away from her own,
and drifting in from the kitchen the smell of buttermilk scones
Was it the same lifetime

My kids were the ones making noise on steps,
The arduous affixing of small-gauge track to plywood;
or before, the pastel tableau of stuffed animals, all dressed
up for the party and the new stuffie Santa left?

A color-coded thread goes further back, where I
as only child imagined a numinous cloud come out of sky
the night all nature stopped— all stores closed—
which gave the cookie left on the plate a special tinge,
a thing I could close my sleepy mind around

the actual opening of gifts always a letdown
The story come apart in the torn foil and loosed bows,
a consciousness bludgeoned by *things*,
as if the snow globe got dropped and shattered yearly,
detritus in the nullifying war between Real or Not,

Christmas sloughed off by the rest of the calendar.
in the everyday slipshod bash of Reality Myth
the Prince of Stories got disappeared

Until children came into the house
bringing Form to join with Story
the fine print instructions I had missed
on the back of each gift,
let the impulse to give
be expressed in a story
which is Form to the giver
who gets from the giving
the subtle understanding
of how to receive

Dream within Dream

I am driving a car with three other people in it, a man and two
women. We may be fleeing someone. On the highway, we drive
through a fresh pile of goose dropping about four feet high. Later
at a restaurant, I ask my passengers if they weren't suspicious of
that pile—How did it get there? When? But nobody seems to
know what I'm talking about. Then I understand: that was my
dream. No one else was having that dream. They didn't even
know they were riding with me in a car.

Hoppy

There is a park deep in the Adirondacks— or maybe the Catskills—
where you can check out an exotic animal like a library book
and keep it with you for as long as you're in the park.
I go there with my high school English teachers Olive and Esther,
who gave me Sophocles and Shakespeare, Yeats, Eliot and
Lawrence and Blake

I hang out with Hoppy, who looks like a child's toy dinosaur,
the size of a Bernese mountain dog, with big sensitive eyes
but when it's time to leave, I can't get him to come back.
Every time I call "Hoppy!" he starts toward me, then hides.

The park people don't seem too worried. Olive and Esther are
cheery as always,
ready to go. "He may already have gone to where he is supposed
to be," they say.
—May have? I say. I need to know for sure. They just roll their eyes,
look at each other, like *when will he wake up?* I didn't know
how then, I tell them
when I waken, across the dark divide. How I love them.

Going to New Zealand

"The most sublime act is to set another before you."
                                                    William Blake

"We go to great lengths to construct a self for our friends. But if
we didn't do that, they would be our friends anyway."
                                                    Ron Harrington

I've known you for a long time
but I never set you before me
now you say you're going to New Zealand
and I follow you out the door for a while

we always valued each other's conversation
You're not beautiful but friendly and good
I watched you leave the restaurant
then followed you a few steps out the door

I felt a warmth each time we came together
a soft light sure, unclouded, so true it was hard to see
There's a guy friend with you, not your boyfriend
I wonder if he's going to New Zealand too

The presence of friendly faces in homeostasis,
(which Damasio says means more than to endure, but to prevail),
those who exalt you just by sitting across from you
letting you be a constellation in their sky

It's not that they have the content of your actions in their minds
they're not here for your achievements or shriveled moments,

they just connect the dots and affirm
the living pattern that you are.

Now you say you're going to New Zealand
how long have we been this way, good friend
I follow you out the door for a while
till I realize I probably won't see you again.

Varieties of Light

Taking a walk down the street with my wife, late;
full moon over the river, its luster thinned
by lights on our block   porch lights   yard lights
motion sensors   Christmas lights
          Old Solstice repurposed
lights the eyes reflect but do not radiate
that envy the moon its original coldness

In dark morning I waken,
hustle down to the lake for sunup
dawn sky clear over blue Ontario's shore
water is quiet till you get
far enough out on the pier
so lake whispers on both sides
high overhead
a vapor trail's curled wisp
catches the light
of the approaching Guest

a woman who has just
gotten out of bed stands by the rail
with her cell phone aimed
I stop walking and look to the west
where shifting languorous darkness awaits
then turn and fix my eyes on the glow

there is pink, and some disturbed shuffling of colors
then no color any more but the popping of a deep
red sexual eye whose gaze I return until I can't.

Below a double reflection appears and where did
those ducks come from, not there a few seconds ago
till one of them throws its head back
and pitches forward to vanish,
the others following suit, all emerging upriver
and I see they aren't ducks but mergansers, cruising
quietly up the channel in the shadowy foreground of sunrise,
having beaten the ducks and the gulls to the good stuff

Universal Face

in the dark winter of the coronavirus

Heaven is walking on a busy street in a big city.

I've been reading Chekov
How rich and meaningful my life is.
I see how what touches my heart
can be carried in the palm of my hand
and disassembled to be analyzed and adored
How the presence of others comforts me
and assures me I am on a continuum

I see a driver getting out of a truck to deliver a package.
He looks familiar. How could I know him? I've never
been in this city. Perhaps he has the universal
face of drivers everywhere, We get on a crowded bus, but

but not to go somewhere. My friend is looking
for a piece of lost luggage. He hands the driver a slip of paper.
The driver looks as if he might know where it is.
We get back off while he goes somewhere to look for it.
He does not look like the other driver, I know
because I can see his whole face.